*Profiles of the Presidents*

# WOODROW WILSON

★ ★ ★

*Profiles of the Presidents*

# WOODROW WILSON

*by Robert Green*

Content Adviser: Lucinda Cooke, Director of Education, Woodrow Wilson Birthplace Foundation, Staunton, Virginia

Reading Adviser: Dr. Linda D. Labbo, Department of Reading Education, College of Education, The University of Georgia

COMPASS POINT BOOKS ✦ MINNEAPOLIS, MINNESOTA

Compass Point Books
3109 West 50th Street, #115
Minneapolis, MN 55410

Visit Compass Point Books on the Internet at *www.compasspointbooks.com*
or e-mail your request to *custserv@compasspointbooks.com*

Editors: E. Russell Primm, Emily J. Dolbear, Melissa McDaniel, and Catherine Neitge
Photo Researchers: Image Select International and Svetlana Zhurkina
Photo Selector: Linda S. Koutris
Designer/Page Production: The Design Lab/Les Tranby
Cartographer: XNR Productions, Inc.

**Library of Congress Cataloging-in-Publication Data**
Green, Robert, 1969–
    Woodrow Wilson / by Robert Green.
       p. cm. — (Profiles of the presidents)
Summary: Biography of the twenty-eighth president of United States, discussing his personal life, education, and political career. Includes bibliographical references (p. ) and index.
  ISBN 0-7565-0274-8 (hardcover)
  1. Wilson, Woodrow, 1856–1924—Juvenile literature. 2. Presidents—United States—Biography—Juvenile literature. [1. Wilson, Woodrow, 1856–1924. 2. Presidents.] I. Title. II. Series.
  E767 .G86 2003
  973.91'3'092—dc21                                   2002010050

# Table of Contents

★　★　★

★

*NOTE: In this book, words that are defined in the glossary are in* **bold** *the first time they appear in the text.*

# An Example for the World

★   ★   ★

**M**any Americans believe that the United States has a special role in the world. President Woodrow Wilson was one of them.

Wilson was the son of a minister. His father taught him strong moral beliefs. He also taught him how to keep a crowd riveted when he was speaking.

*Woodrow Wilson on ▶ the campaign trail*

◀ *When Wilson delivered his sermonlike speeches, he was trying to make America morally stronger.*

Other politicians did not always like Wilson's high moral view of his own actions. So Wilson took his ideas directly to the people. President Wilson's speeches were like sermons. His goal was to strengthen America's morals. He wanted to hold up the nation as an example for the world. "The force of America," he said, "is the force of moral **principle**."

Wilson opposed war more than anything. He couldn't control events in Europe, however, and World War I (1914-1918) broke out there while he was president.

Wilson proved to be an able wartime leader. From the day the United States entered the war, though, Wilson looked constantly toward peace. He dreamed of creating a lasting peace. He wanted to live in a world where people would be safe—a world where nations solved their problems through discussion rather than violence. This would be both his greatest hope and his greatest disappointment.

American troops ▶ amid the rubble of a building during World War I

# The Making of an Idealist

★ ★ ★

Thomas Woodrow Wilson was born in Staunton, Virginia, on December 28, 1856. He was the third child born to Joseph Ruggles Wilson and Jessie Woodrow Wilson.

Wilson's father was a teacher and minister. He was originally from Ohio but had moved to Virginia to become the minister of a Presbyterian church. Jessie Woodrow was from England, where her own father was a Presbyterian minister.

▼ Wilson's parents, Joseph and Jessie

Woodrow's father taught his son to honor God. He also taught him to be curious and to love learning.

His father often took Woodrow on walks. They would visit stores and factories, warehouses and banks. All the while, his father would explain how the machines worked and what the people were doing. Woodrow's father could be stern and demanding, but he was also fun and inspiring.

*The Battle of ▼ Gettysburg resulted in heavy losses for both Northern and Southern troops during the Civil War.*

Young Woodrow had found his hero in his very own home.

In 1861, when Woodrow was just five years old, the American Civil War between the Northern and Southern states began. At that time, the Wilsons were living in Augusta, Georgia, in the Deep South.

Augusta saw little fighting during the war. Joseph Wilson's church, however, was used as a hospital for Southern troops. Woodrow saw the young men with their horrible wounds, and he began to understand the horror of war.

The Wilsons moved to Columbia, South Carolina, in 1870, five years after the Civil War had ended with the South's defeat. The city of Augusta had not been damaged in the war, but Northern troops had laid waste to Columbia. The scars still showed. This gave Woodrow a good look at the destruction of war. It was not something he would forget.

▾ *The Wilson family's home in Columbia, South Carolina*

Woodrow did not begin attending school until after the war ended. When he first went to school, he didn't do well. He found the drills boring. He also had trouble reading. Although Woodrow's parents often read to him, he was slow to learn to read himself. He did not really learn until he was about eleven years old. Today, historians think that Wilson may have had a reading problem called dyslexia. People with dyslexia sometimes see words and letters backward or in a different order than they are printed on the page. Once Woodrow figured out how to read, it became one of his great loves. He was almost never without a book.

*Wilson (seated) ▶ found reading a challenge at first but worked to overcome his difficulties.*

Woodrow had a lot of fun as a boy. He played baseball and football, and he played them well. He knew everything about ships and their flags, and he liked adventure stories.

Yet there was a seriousness about Woodrow that set him apart. He had a dignity

that other boys lacked. His parents were sure he would fol-
low in his father's footsteps and become a minister. Woodrow had other ideas.

He believed that God had chosen him to govern. He
had watched as the nation had been nearly torn apart during the Civil War. Woodrow wanted to guide the United
States toward what he saw as its great **destiny.**

▾ *Wilson had
witnessed the
horrible destruction
of the Civil War.*

*Davidson College in the 1870s*

Woodrow Wilson began college when he was just sixteen years old. He left home to attend Davidson College in North Carolina. Wilson was not happy at the small college. He was very shy and had trouble getting used to being away from his family. He grew terribly homesick.

He also grew ill. He often suffered from bad colds and coughing fits. When he returned home in June, he begged his parents not to make him go back to Davidson in the fall. Wilson spent the next year studying at home. Then his parents decided that he should continue his formal education.

So, in 1875, Woodrow Wilson entered Princeton University, which was then known as the College of New Jersey. Although he found his schoolwork difficult the first year, he also made a lot of friends. By his second year at Princeton, he was thriving. He started a debating club, in which students practiced making formal arguments. In time, he became managing editor of the student newspaper. He would later call his time at Princeton "magical years."

At Princeton, Wilson studied government, economics, and literature. He believed that these studies would lead him to greatness. He dreamed of the career he might have

◄ *When Wilson returned to college, he attended Princeton.*

*Wilson as a ▶ young lawyer*

one day. He even handed out name cards that read, "Thomas Woodrow Wilson, Senator from Virginia."

Wilson thought hard about how to get started on the road to politics. Finally, he settled on going to law school at the University of Virginia. He didn't enjoy law school, though. He found it dull and tiresome. Rather than studying his law books, he read the history books that he loved so much. He also did well in the school's debating society.

In time, Wilson decided to drop out of law school, but he didn't give up on law entirely. He finished his studies from home. Then he took the bar exam, the test that lawyers have to pass to be allowed to practice law. Although he didn't have a law degree, Wilson had become a lawyer.

weak. He thought the president should be more involved in guiding new laws through Congress.

*Congressional Government* brought Wilson to the attention of politicians and political thinkers. He had begun to make his start in politics. During that same good year, he married Ellen Axson.

◄ *Woodrow Wilson and Ellen Axson Wilson*

# Return to Princeton

★ ★ ★

In 1886, Woodrow Wilson earned a doctor's degree from Johns Hopkins University. The young boy who had trouble learning to read now had a Ph.D.—the most advanced degree there is. To this day, he is the only president to have earned a doctorate.

Wilson took a job teaching at Bryn Mawr, a famous women's college. He longed, however, to teach a "class of men."

Two years later, he got his wish. He took a job at Wesleyan University in Middletown, Connecticut. There he taught his students to love politics. He also coached one of the school's most successful football teams.

Being a professor suited Wilson. He spent countless hours doing the things he loved—thinking, lecturing, and writing. Words began to flow from his pen. He wrote more studies of government, a history of the

◀ *Wilson taught only
female students at
Bryn Mawr.*

American Civil War, and
began his book called
*History of the American
People.* He also wrote
articles for leading maga-
zines, including the
*Atlantic Monthly.*

◀ *Wilson returned
to Princeton as
a professor*

In 1890, Wilson returned
to Princeton to become a professor
there. He had loved going to college at
Princeton. Now he proved to be a good professor.

Wilson's reputation grew. Soon he was getting offers to become the president of other universities. One school that wanted him was the University of Virginia, in his home state. Wilson was loyal to Princeton, however, and stayed. In 1902, Wilson was named the president of Princeton.

Wilson was president of Princeton for eight years. During that time, he tried to **reform** the school. He believed that Princeton should be producing well-rounded students of the highest quality. Early on, he changed the

*Wilson received ▸ several offers to head other universities, but he accepted the post of president of Princeton in 1902.*

classes that students took. He had new buildings constructed so there would be more room for classes. He also hired many energetic young professors so the students would be in smaller classes.

Over time, Wilson's plans for changing the school

reached further. Some teachers and former students grew angry at what he suggested. Toward the end of his time as Princeton's president, he got involved in two major arguments over the future of the university.

The first argument involved Wilson's idea to get rid of the university's eating clubs. These clubs had been established by wealthy students. Many students were not allowed to join the clubs. Wilson called this snobbery and thought it was bad for student life. Instead, he thought that all students should live and eat together. Then they might share what they learned with one another, and no students would be left out.

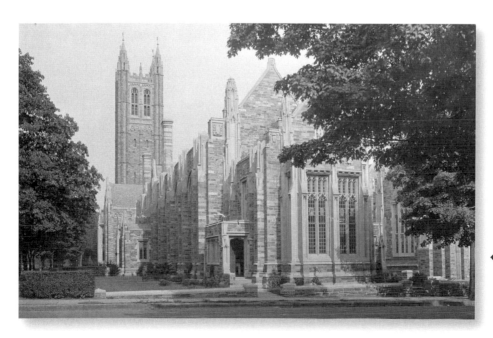

◀ *One of Princeton's dining halls during the early 1900s*

Many Princeton graduates had fond memories of the eating clubs, however. They wanted to keep the tradition. They were outraged when they heard that Wilson planned to get rid of the clubs. Many complained. In the end, Wilson lost the battle.

Wilson was furious. Defeat always seemed to surprise him. Perhaps this was because he was so sure he was right. He thought about quitting as the university president, but he decided to remain in his position.

Wilson's second big battle at Princeton erupted over where a new graduate school would be built. The university had been given a lot of money to build the new

Buildings on the ▶
campus of
Princeton's
graduate school

school at a site away from the college. Wilson rejected the idea. He believed that the older students would have a good influence on the younger students. He insisted that the graduate school should be on the existing campus.

In this fight, Wilson ran up against the head of the graduate school, Andrew F. West. He was every bit as stubborn as Wilson. West demanded that the graduate school be off the campus. The fight became personal. Both men had supporters among the professors. In 1910, West's plan was approved—the graduate school would be separate from the college.

After losing this battle, Wilson believed that the honorable thing for him to do was to leave Princeton. Fortunately, the political career that he had long dreamed of was just around the corner.

◄ *Andrew West, the head of Princeton's graduate school and Wilson's opponent in the debate over connected campuses*

# Crusade for Reform

★  ★  ★

**N**ever did a man so quickly land on his feet. The timing of Wilson's exit from Princeton couldn't have been better. The year was 1910, and the Democratic Party of New Jersey was looking for someone to run for governor.

The editor of *Harper's Magazine,* Colonel George Harvey, was already interested in Wilson. Harvey had published some of Wilson's articles in his magazine. He believed that Wilson would be a good leader for the Democrats. He convinced James Smith, the leader of the New Jersey Democratic Party, that Woodrow Wilson should be the Democratic **candidate** for governor.

Smith offered to help Wilson win the election. Wilson accepted, as long as he did not have to promise any favors in return. Smith agreed, although he secretly had plans of his own. With Smith's support, Wilson won easily. Smith believed that he had his own man in the governor's mansion. Wilson, however, believed that he had been elected to serve the will of the people.

Wilson and Smith clashed right away. Wilson had always opposed the way local political party organizations would make backroom deals. He would have none of it. To make this point, he blocked Smith's own **nomination** for the New Jersey state **legislature.**

Wilson was committed to trying to reform the American political system. Luckily, the American public was in the mood for change.

◄ *The Princeton home where Wilson and his family lived while he served as governor of New Jersey*

Governor ▶
Woodrow Wilson
(seated)

Governor Wilson kept constant pressure on the New Jersey legislature to pass reform laws. He hounded politicians, both Republican and Democrat. Wilson also took the fight to the people. He gave speeches around the state to drum up support for reform.

Wilson had stunning success from these efforts. He succeeded in changing the way candidates for the New Jersey state legislature were chosen. No longer would candidates be chosen by the parties. Now they would have to win primary elections. This weakened the power of the local party organizations.

Wilson also worked to pass other reform laws to help ordinary people. In the early twentieth century,

many big companies had become very powerful. Some
were so powerful that they were able to drive smaller
companies out of business. They were now **monopolies.**
Both Republicans and Democrats wanted to limit the
power of these giant corporations.

Wilson won support for laws that made monopolies
illegal in New Jersey. He also helped pass measures that
prevented electric companies from charging the public too
much. In addition, he pushed through a law that protect-
ed workers who were injured on the job. This law made
sure that the workers would not lose their livelihood.

▾ *This political
cartoon depicts
the overwhelming
power of monopolies.*

Most politicians are lucky if they pass one or two key items during one term in office. In a single two-year term, Wilson passed nearly all of his reform ideas. Wilson had long believed that a governor or a president should steer proposed laws through the legislature, and he showed exactly how that could be done. He also proved that a professor of politics could be an able politician.

Factories like this steel mill were often dangerous in the early 1900s, but Wilson supported a law to help workers in case they were injured.

# The New Freedom

★ ★ ★

**W**oodrow Wilson's success as governor of New Jersey brought him national attention. Because of his strong record of reform, he became the Democratic candidate for president in 1912.

It turned out to be one of the most unusual presidential elections in U.S. history. President William Howard Taft, a Republican,

▲ Wilson's Republican opponent, William Howard Taft

was running for reelection. Taft might have had a chance if former president Theodore Roosevelt hadn't jumped into the race. Roosevelt left the Republican Party to run as a third-party candidate.

Wilson succeeded ▶
in becoming leader
of the nation after
a short but eventful
career in state politics.

Roosevelt's bid for the presidency stole the thunder of the Republicans. The Republican votes were split between Taft and Roosevelt. As a result, Wilson, the Democrat, won.

Just two years after entering politics, Woodrow Wilson achieved his highest goal. He became the president of the United States.

A month after Wilson took office on March 4, 1913, he gave a speech before Congress. He wanted to make it clear to the lawmakers that "the president is a person, not a mere department of the Government."

Wilson was warning Congress that he meant to lead. Right away, he started promoting what he called his New Freedom program. Wilson wanted to pass laws that would make the United States fairer for working people. He also wanted to pass laws that would limit the power of large companies.

His first goal was to lower tariffs. He believed that these taxes on goods brought into the country helped large U.S. companies by raising the price of foreign goods. This meant that consumers had to pay more if they bought foreign goods. After a long fight, Wilson managed to get the law passed.

◀ *Wilson was eager to improve life for working people like these North Carolina cotton mill employees.*

In his first year in office, Wilson also changed the U.S. banking system. He pushed through a law establishing the Federal Reserve. This organization works to keep the nation's economy stable.

Wilson's third great New Freedom law was the Clayton Anti-Trust Act of 1914. This law outlawed monopolies. It enables the national government to keep a close watch over big businesses and make sure they are playing by the rules.

Wilson seemed to be replaying his success as governor of New Jersey. He kept Congress busy and prodded members of both parties to support his ideas.

*The signing of the Federal Reserve Act in 1913*

In public, President Wilson was a serious figure. At home, however, he relaxed a little. He loved to read poetry and act out plays with his family. Two of his three daughters were married while he was president. One of them, Eleanor, married Wilson's secretary of the treasury, William McAdoo.

These early years of Wilson's presidency were happy. Then, in August 1914, his world was plunged into darkness.

◄ *William and Eleanor McAdoo with one of their daughters*

◄ *Wilson experienced political success during his first few years in office.*

# The Long Road to War

★ ★ ★

On August 6, 1914, President Woodrow Wilson suddenly found himself a widower. That day, his wife died from a kidney disease. On hearing the news, Wilson stared blankly out a window at the White House. "Oh my God," he cried. "What am I to do?"

Ellen Axson Wilson ▶ at the White House with her daughters (from left), Eleanor, Margaret, and Jessie

The news of his wife's death came just after war broke out in Europe. Many nations would get involved in this conflict. Among the most powerful were Great Britain and France on one side, and Germany on the other. Wilson was determined to keep the United States out of the war. "We must be **impartial** in thought as well as action," he told Americans. They were glad to hear him say that. Few of them wanted anything to do with the war. Wilson hoped to keep the United States strictly neutral. It wouldn't support either side.

◀ *German soldiers advance during a battle on August 7, 1914.*

Wilson (left) and Edith Bolling Galt

The following year, Wilson became friends with a woman named Edith Bolling Galt, who was herself a widow. Galt was lively and intelligent. It seemed that for the first time since Ellen Wilson had died, there was laughter in the White House. By the end of the year, Wilson and Galt were married.

Meanwhile, the war in Europe had bogged down. Neither side could claim victory. On May 7, 1915, a German submarine sank a British ship called the *Lusitania*. Among the dead were 128 Americans. Wilson was shocked. He thought firing at unarmed ships was savage.

"All the News That's Fit to Print."

## The New York Times.

THE WEATHER

VOL. LXIV...NO. 20,923. NEW YORK, SATURDAY, MAY 8, 1915.—TWENTY-FOUR PAGES. ONE CENT

### LUSITANIA SUNK BY A SUBMARINE, PROBABLY 1,000 DEAD; TWICE TORPEDOED OFF IRISH COAST; SINKS IN 15 MINUTES; AMERICANS ABOARD INCLUDED VANDERBILT AND FROHMAN; WASHINGTON BELIEVES THAT A GRAVE CRISIS IS AT HAND

*◄ The front page of the* New York Times *reported the sinking of the* Lusitania.

*▲ A truck with campaign posters encouraging Americans to reelect Wilson in 1916*

Wilson tried to convince the Germans of this. By the spring of 1916, the Germans had backed off and were no longer firing at unarmed ships. Americans were grateful that their nation hadn't been dragged into the conflict. Wilson ran for reelection with the **slogan,** "He Kept Us Out of War."

Wilson's reelection in 1916 gave him confidence. He wanted to act as a peacemaker. He called for a "peace without victory." Neither side was willing to accept the idea, however.

Germany wanted to starve Great Britain into giving up. Because Great Britain is an island, the Germans thought this might be possible if they destroyed the ships that delivered food and war supplies. To do this, Germany would have to destroy neutral ships as well.

*A German submarine surfaces during World War I.*

The Germans announced that they were willing to attack unarmed ships that were supplying Great Britain.

They knew this might bring the United States into the war, but they thought it was worth the gamble. The Germans thought the Americans would take so long preparing for the war that they wouldn't make much difference on the battlefield. The Germans, however, misjudged President Wilson's determination. They also misjudged the United States' ability to equip an army quickly.

On April 2, 1917, Wilson asked Congress to declare war. His peace efforts had failed. "The world must be made safe for democracy," he declared.

◄ *Wilson reading the declaration of war to Congress in April 1917*

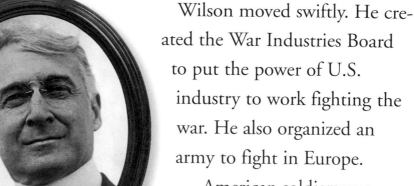

Bernard Baruch ▶
*headed the War
Industries Board
for Wilson.*

Wilson moved swiftly. He created the War Industries Board to put the power of U.S. industry to work fighting the war. He also organized an army to fight in Europe.

American soldiers were soon fighting alongside British and French soldiers on the battlefields of France. They arrived in time to beat back the last great German attack. They also gave some much-needed hope to the British and French, who were worn out from four years of fighting.

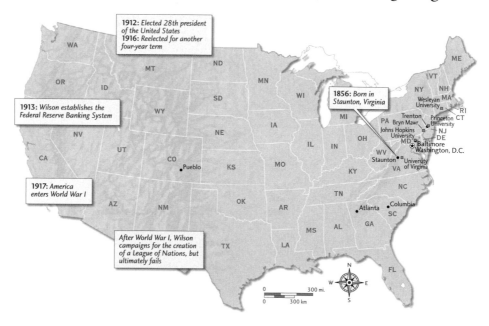

1912: *Elected 28th president of the United States*
1916: *Reelected for another four-year term*

1913: *Wilson establishes the Federal Reserve Banking System*

1856: *Born in Staunton, Virginia*

1917: *America enters World War I*

After World War I, Wilson *campaigns for the creation of a League of Nations, but ultimately fails*

# A Man of Peace

★ ★ ★

Even before the war ended, President Wilson had an outline for the peace settlement. His plan included Fourteen Points. They ranged from settling conflicts over borders to creating an international organization called the League of Nations. The purpose of this organization was to settle future disputes peacefully, through discussion. Wilson dreamed of a peace that would not only end the current war but also prevent future conflicts.

By the autumn of 1918, the German war effort had run out of steam. Wilson convinced Germany to put an end to the fighting. World War I had ended.

▼ Lloyd George of England (left), Vittorio Orlando of Italy, Georges Clemenceau of France, and President Woodrow Wilson, just before the start of the Paris Peace Conference

A peace treaty was to be worked out at the Paris Peace Conference of 1919. Wilson sailed to Europe to represent the United States at the conference and to work to create the League of Nations.

When Wilson arrived in Europe, he was greeted by large crowds of cheering supporters. Newspapers said he had saved Europe. In the U.S. president, Europeans saw hope for a lasting peace. This was the high point of Wilson's presidency. For many, he had become a living symbol of justice and peace.

*Wilson (center) and other members of the American delegation at the peace conference* ▶

British and French officials at the peace conference
took a different view. In their minds, Germany had started
the war, so Germany should pay for it. Also, the French
wanted to **occupy** part of Germany. The British and the
French had secretly drawn up plans to divide former
German **colonies** and large parts of the Middle East
between themselves.

Wilson strongly disagreed with the British and French
officials. He spent six months in Europe working for his
Fourteen Points.

▼ *President Wilson
(shown riding
beside French
president Raymond
Poincaré) stayed
in Europe for
several months.*

"Had the Treaty of Paris been drafted solely by the American experts, it would have been one of the wisest as well as most scientific documents ever devised," wrote Harold Nicolson, a British official at the peace conference. Instead, the treaty demanded that Germany make huge payments for the war. This made the German people bitter. In time, it would leave the nation in financial ruins.

Still, Wilson was successful in some of his efforts. Great Britain and France agreed to the creation of the League of Nations. They also agreed to put some former German colonies on the road toward independence.

*Henry Cabot Lodge* ▾

Wilson returned to the United States, where he still had to convince the U.S. Congress to agree to the treaty. He found Congress angry and unhappy. In 1918, the Republicans had won both houses of Congress. A group of Republicans led by Senator Henry Cabot Lodge of Massachusetts was determined to defeat the peace treaty.

Lodge objected to language that said the United States would have to aid other nations in times of war. He believed that the United States should take care of itself, not get involved in other countries' problems.

In September 1919, Wilson traveled around the nation to drum up support for the treaty and the League of Nations. He gave speeches in thirty cities. The trip was exhausting. One night in Pueblo, Colorado, he collapsed.

Wilson was rushed back to Washington, where he suffered a **stroke.** He was near death and partly **paralyzed.** For five months, the U.S. government had no leader. Wilson's wife, Edith, and his doctor, Cary Grayson, carefully controlled who saw him. They allowed only a few people to visit him. They also hid how bad his condition was.

◄ *Wilson gave several speeches to rally American support for the peace treaty.*

Slowly, Wilson recovered. He was never the same again, however. He grew angry more easily. He was even less willing to **compromise.**

Senator Lodge told Wilson he would sign the peace treaty only if the United States were not bound to honor pledges to go to war. Wilson refused. He would not budge from his stand, nor would Senator Lodge. The disagreement between the two men became personal. They came to intensely dislike each other.

*Wilson considered ▼ running for a third term despite how ill he was.*

In the end, the Senate rejected the treaty. Wilson's dream of gaining U.S. support for the League of Nations faded.

People in other parts of the world valued Wilson's peacemaking efforts more. He was awarded the 1919 Nobel Peace Prize for his work in helping to create the League of Nations.

As sick as he was, Wilson thought about running for another term as president. He thought this would give the country the chance to decide about the treaty and the League of Nations. In the end, however, he decided not to run.

Wilson's career was finished. He retired to his house on S Street in Washington, D.C. He lived there quietly until his death on February 3, 1924.

Wilson had been devastated by losing the treaty fight. The American people had rejected his vision for future peace. It was partly his own doing, however, because he was unable to compromise. He could not accept that his fellow citizens did not agree with his vision of their country's future.

◄ *A crowd greets former president Woodrow Wilson.*

Between 1939 and 1945, the world would see another great war. Many people believe that World War II was caused in part by the harsh terms forced on Germany at the end of World War I. By the end of World War II, many Americans understood that the United States had an important role to play in the world. The United States would become a leading member of the United Nations. Like the old League of Nations, the UN is an international organization that works to settle disputes peacefully.

Woodrow Wilson's dream had survived him.

The New York ▶
headquarters for
the United Nations

# GLOSSARY

★ ★ ★

**candidate**—someone running for office in an election

**colonies**—territories ruled by people from another country

**compromise**—an agreement that is reached by both sides giving up part of what they want

**destiny**—special purpose

**graduate school**—a school offering advanced degrees for students who have already completed college

**impartial**—not favoring either side

**legislature**—the part of government that makes or changes laws

**monopolies**—companies that control an entire industry

**nomination**—chosen as a candidate for office

**occupy**—to keep troops in a defeated country after a war

**paralyzed**—unable to move

**principle**—a basic law or rule of conduct

**reform**—an improvement, or the correcting of something that is unsatisfactory

**slogan**—a phrase used to capture public attention in a campaign

**stroke**—a problem in the brain causing a sudden loss of the ability to feel or move

# WOODROW WILSON'S LIFE AT A GLANCE

★ ★ ★

## PERSONAL

**Nickname:** Schoolmaster in Politics

**Born:** December 28, 1856

**Birthplace:** Staunton, Virginia

**Father's name:** Joseph Ruggles Wilson

**Mother's name:** Jessie Janet Woodrow Wilson

**Education:** Graduated from College of New Jersey (Princeton University) in 1879; earned a Ph.D. from Johns Hopkins University in 1886

**Wives' names:** Ellen Louise Axson Wilson (1860–1914); Edith Bolling Galt Wilson (1872–1961)

**Married:** June 24, 1885; December 18, 1915

**Children:** Margaret Woodrow Wilson (1886–1944); Jessie Woodrow Wilson (1887–1933); Eleanor Randolph Wilson (1889–1967)

**Died:** February 3, 1924, in Washington, D.C.

**Buried:** The National Cathedral in Washington, D.C.

# PUBLIC

| | |
|---|---|
| **Occupation before presidency:** | Teacher, public official |
| **Occupation after presidency:** | Retired |
| **Military service:** | None |
| **Other government positions:** | Governor of New Jersey |
| **Political party:** | Democrat |
| **Vice president:** | Thomas R. Marshall (1913–1921) |
| **Dates in office:** | March 4, 1913–March 3, 1921 |
| **Presidential opponents:** | William Howard Taft (Republican) and Theodore Roosevelt (Progressive), 1912; Charles Evans Hughes (Republican), 1916 |
| **Number of votes (Electoral College):** | 6,296,547 of 13,901,838 (435 of 531), 1912; 9,127,695 of 17,661,202 (277 of 531), 1916 |
| **Selected Writings:** | *Congressional Government: A Study in American Politics* (1885); *A History of the American People* (5 vols., 1902); *Constitutional Government in the United States* (1908) |

## Woodrow Wilson's Cabinet

*Secretary of state:*
William Jennings Bryan (1913–1915)
Robert Lansing (1915–1920)
Bainbridge Colby (1920–1921)

*Secretary of the treasury:*
William G. McAdoo (1913–1918)
Carter Glass (1918–1920)
David F. Houston (1920–1921)

*Secretary of war:*
Lindley M. Garrison (1913–1916)
Newton D. Baker (1916–1921)

*Attorney general:*
James C. McReynolds (1913–1914)
Thomas W. Gregory (1914–1919)
Alexander M. Palmer (1919–1921)

*Postmaster general:*
Albert S. Burleson (1913–1921)

*Secretary of the navy:*
Josephus Daniels (1913 1921)

*Secretary of the interior:*
Franklin K. Lane (1913–1920)
John B. Payne (1920–1921)

*Secretary of agriculture:*
David F. Houston (1913–1920)
Edwin T. Meredith (1920–1921)

*Secretary of commerce:*
William C. Redfield (1913–1919)
Joshua W. Alexander (1919–1921)

*Secretary of labor:*
William B. Wilson (1913–1921)

# WOODROW WILSON'S LIFE AND TIMES

★ ★ ★

| WILSON'S LIFE | WORLD EVENTS |
|---|---|

**December 28, Wilson is born in Staunton, Virginia** — 1856

**1858** — English scientist Charles Darwin presents his theory of evolution

**1860**

**1860** — Austrian composer Gustav Mahler is born in Kalischt (now in Austria)

**1865** — Lewis Carroll writes *Alice's Adventures in Wonderland*

**1869** — The transcontinental railroad across the United States is completed (below)

**1870**

**Enters Princeton University (above), then called College of New Jersey** — 1875

## WILSON'S LIFE

## WORLD EVENTS

1876   The Battle of the Little Bighorn is a victory for Native Americans defending their homes in the West against General George Custer (right)

**1880**

Alexander Graham Bell uses the first telephone to speak to his assistant, Thomas Watson

Passes the bar exam   1882

1882   Thomas Edison builds a power station

1884   Mark Twain (below) publishes *The Adventures of Huckleberry Finn*

June 24, marries Ellen   1885
Louise Axson (below)

## WILSON'S LIFE

Receives a Ph.D. from
Johns Hopkins
University    1886

Begins teaching at
Wesleyan University    1888

Begins teaching at
Princeton University    1890

Becomes president of
Princeton University    1892

Elected governor of
New Jersey    1910

**1890**

**1900**

## WORLD EVENTS

1886   Grover Cleveland
dedicates the Statue of
Liberty in New York

Bombing in
Haymarket Square,
Chicago, due to labor
unrest (below)

1891   The Roman Catholic
Church publishes the
encyclical *Rerum
Novarum*, which
supports the rights
of labor

1893   Women gain voting
privileges in New
Zealand, the first
country to take
such a step

1909   The National
Association for the
Advancement of
Colored People
(NAACP) is founded

## WILSON'S LIFE

## WORLD EVENTS

| Presidential Election Results: | | Popular Votes | Electoral Votes |
|---|---|---|---|
| **1912** | Woodrow Wilson | 6,296,547 | 435 |
| | Theodore Roosevelt | 4,118,571 | 88 |
| | William Howard Taft | 3,486,720 | 8 |

**1913** Signs the Underwood Tariff Act reducing tariffs

Signs the Federal Reserve Act establishing the Federal Reserve Banking System

**1913** Henry Ford begins to use standard assembly lines to produce automobiles

**1914** The Federal Trade Commission is established to stop unfair business practices

Signs the Clayton Anti-Trust Act to help limit the power of big business

August 6, Ellen Wilson dies

**1914** Archduke Francis Ferdinand is assassinated, launching World War I

The Panama Canal opens to traffic

| WILSON'S LIFE | WORLD EVENTS |
|---|---|

**WILSON'S LIFE**

December 18, 1915
marries Edith
Bolling Galt

**WORLD EVENTS**

1915   May 7, a German
submarine sinks
the *Lusitania*

| Presidential Election Results: | | Popular Votes | Electoral Votes |
|---|---|---|---|
| 1916 | Woodrow Wilson | 9,127,695 | 277 |
| | Charles Evans Hughes | 8,533,507 | 254 |

1916   German-born physicist
Albert Einstein (below),
publishes his general
theory of relativity

April 6, the United 1917
States declares war
on Germany

1917   February, Germany
begins unlimited
submarine warfare

Vladimir Ilyich Lenin
and Leon Trotsky lead
Bolsheviks in a rebellion
against the czars in
Russia during the
October Revolution

"Buffalo Bill" Cody dies
in Denver, Colorado

## WILSON'S LIFE

## WORLD EVENTS

January 8, delivers his
Fourteen Points to
Congress as a guide for
the peace settlement

**1918**

November 11, World
War I ends

World War I peace
conference begins at
Versailles, France

**1919**

October 2, suffers a
stroke, leaving him
partly paralyzed

December 10, receives
the Nobel Peace Prize
for his work on the
League of Nations

**1919** Boston Red Sox player
Babe Ruth (above) hits a
record twenty-nine
home runs

Prohibition is adopted
as the 18th Amendment,
outlawing the sale of
alcoholic beverages in
the United States

**1920**

**1923** French actress Sarah
Bernhardt (below) dies

February 3, dies in
Washington, D.C.

**1924**

# UNDERSTANDING WOODROW WILSON AND HIS PRESIDENCY

★ ★ ★

## IN THE LIBRARY

Joseph, Paul. *Woodrow Wilson.* Minneapolis: Abdo Publishing, 2001.

Holden, Henry M. *Woodrow Wilson.* Berkeley Heights, N.J.: MyReportlinks.com Books, 2003.

Rogers, James T. *Woodrow Wilson: Visionary for Peace.* New York: Facts on File, 1997.

Schraff, Anne. *Woodrow Wilson.* Springfield, N.J.: Enslow, 1998.

## ON THE WEB

For more information on *Woodrow Wilson*, use FactHound to track down Web sites related to this book.

1. Go to *www.facthound.com*
2. Type in this book ID: 0756502748
3. Click on the *Fetch It* button.

Your trusty FactHound will fetch the best Web sites for you!

## WILSON HISTORIC SITES
## ACROSS THE COUNTRY

**Woodrow Wilson Birthplace**
18-24 North Coalter Street
Staunton, VA 24401
540/885-0897
*http://www.woodrowwilson.org*
To see the house in which Wilson
was born

**The Woodrow Wilson House**
2340 S Street N.W.
Washington, DC 20008
202/387-4062
*http://www.woodrowwilsonhouse.org/*
To visit the only presidential
museum in Washington, D.C., and
the house where Wilson lived after
his presidency

**Woodrow Wilson's Boyhood Home**
1705 Hampton Street
Columbia, SC 29201
803/252-1770
To visit a house where Wilson lived
as a child

# THE U.S. PRESIDENTS
## *(Years in Office)*

★ ★ ★

1. **George Washington**
   (March 4, 1789-March 3, 1797)
2. **John Adams**
   (March 4, 1797-March 3, 1801)
3. **Thomas Jefferson**
   (March 4, 1801-March 3, 1809)
4. **James Madison**
   (March 4, 1809-March 3, 1817)
5. **James Monroe**
   (March 4, 1817-March 3, 1825)
6. **John Quincy Adams**
   (March 4, 1825-March 3, 1829)
7. **Andrew Jackson**
   (March 4, 1829-March 3, 1837)
8. **Martin Van Buren**
   (March 4, 1837-March 3, 1841)
9. **William Henry Harrison**
   (March 6, 1841-April 4, 1841)
10. **John Tyler**
    (April 6, 1841-March 3, 1845)
11. **James K. Polk**
    (March 4, 1845-March 3, 1849)
12. **Zachary Taylor**
    (March 5, 1849-July 9, 1850)
13. **Millard Fillmore**
    (July 10, 1850-March 3, 1853)
14. **Franklin Pierce**
    (March 4, 1853-March 3, 1857)
15. **James Buchanan**
    (March 4, 1857-March 3, 1861)
16. **Abraham Lincoln**
    (March 4, 1861-April 15, 1865)
17. **Andrew Johnson**
    (April 15, 1865-March 3, 1869)

18. **Ulysses S. Grant**
    (March 4, 1869-March 3, 1877)
19. **Rutherford B. Hayes**
    (March 4, 1877-March 3, 1881)
20. **James Garfield**
    (March 4, 1881-Sept 19, 1881)
21. **Chester Arthur**
    (Sept 20, 1881-March 3, 1885)
22. **Grover Cleveland**
    (March 4, 1885-March 3, 1889)
23. **Benjamin Harrison**
    (March 4, 1889-March 3, 1893)
24. **Grover Cleveland**
    (March 4, 1893-March 3, 1897)
25. **William McKinley**
    (March 4, 1897-
    September 14, 1901)
26. **Theodore Roosevelt**
    (September 14, 1901-
    March 3, 1909)
27. **William Howard Taft**
    (March 4, 1909-March 3, 1913)
28. **Woodrow Wilson**
    (March 4, 1913-March 3, 1921)
29. **Warren G. Harding**
    (March 4, 1921-August 2, 1923)
30. **Calvin Coolidge**
    (August 3, 1923-March 3, 1929)
31. **Herbert Hoover**
    (March 4, 1929-March 3, 1933)
32. **Franklin D. Roosevelt**
    (March 4, 1933-April 12, 1945)

33. **Harry S. Truman**
    (April 12, 1945-
    January 20, 1953)
34. **Dwight D. Eisenhower**
    (January 20, 1953-
    January 20, 1961)
35. **John F. Kennedy**
    (January 20, 1961-
    November 22, 1963)
36. **Lyndon B. Johnson**
    (November 22, 1963-
    January 20, 1969)
37. **Richard M. Nixon**
    (January 20, 1969-
    August 9, 1974)
38. **Gerald R. Ford**
    (August 9, 1974-
    January 20, 1977)
39. **James Earl Carter**
    (January 20, 1977-
    January 20, 1981)
40. **Ronald Reagan**
    (January 20, 1981-
    January 20, 1989)
41. **George H. W. Bush**
    (January 20, 1989-
    January 20, 1993)
42. **William Jefferson Clinton**
    (January 20, 1993-
    January 20, 2001)
43. **George W. Bush**
    (January 20, 2001- )

# INDEX

★ ★ ★

## ABOUT THE AUTHOR

Robert Green holds a master's degree in journalism from New York University and a bachelor's degree in English literature from Boston University.

Green is the author of two other titles in this series—*Theodore Roosevelt* and *Richard Nixon*—and of twenty other books for young readers, including *Modern Nations of the World: China* and *Modern Nations of the World: Taiwan.* He has also written biographies of historical figures including Julius Caesar, Cleopatra, and Alexander the Great. Currently, Green lives in Taiwan and is an editor for a Taiwan magazine.